William Francis Taylor

English Reformation

William Francis Taylor

English Reformation

ISBN/EAN: 9783337296025

Printed in Europe, USA, Canada, Australia, Japan

Cover: Foto ©Lupo / pixelio.de

More available books at **www.hansebooks.com**

THE

ENGLISH REFORMATION

SIXTEENTH CENTURY

SIX LECTURES

BY

W. F. TAYLOR, D.D.

*Archdeacon of Liverpool and Vicar of St. Andrews', Aigburth Road,
Toxteth Park*

LIVERPOOL
EDWARD HOWELL CHURCH STREET
LONDON
SIMPKIN, MARSHALL & CO LTD
18,6

PREFACE.

The importance of accurate knowledge as to the nature and extent of the Reformation of the Church of England in the Sixteenth Century, cannot be exaggerated at the present time. Many Church people, both lay and clerical, deny that there was any doctrinal change effected at all at that time; or if any, only of a trifling character: and maintain that the doctrines of the Church are in substantial agreement with the Church of Rome, and the Council of Trent. The late Dr. Pusey held this view, and so, I believe, does Lord Halifax. In the following lectures I have shown that this is not the case, and my object has been to put before the reader, in a brief and accurate manner, the several steps or stages in which the Reformation was effected in this country; *i.e.*—as far as the Church of England is concerned. Those stages were four, and took place under the successive reigns of Henry VIII., Edward VI., Mary, and Elizabeth. I have confined myself strictly, in each lecture, to what was actually accomplished under each sovereign, and nothing beyond.

The result of the long struggle was that after many vicissitudes, the Reformation was firmly established by Elizabeth in 1559, on the Edwardine Settlement, and so continues unto this day. It must, however, be distinctly borne in mind that it was not the First, partially reformed, Prayer Book of Edward which she adopted; but the Second Book, from which every trace of the Mass and the sacrificing priesthood had been carefully expunged. This is expressly stated in the Act of Uniformity, which is found in the large Prayer Book which lies on every reading desk.

The particulars I have mentioned in reference to the successive changes, may be relied upon as strictly accurate; and they prove that, whether right or wrong, the Church of England is thoroughly Protestant in the rejection of all distinctively Roman doctrine and ritual.

W. F. T.

ERRATA.

Page   1, *for* "Lev." *read* "Jer."

  ,,   6, *instead of* 1509, *read* 1409.

  ,, 28,   ,,   1533, ,, 1553.

  ,, 32,   ,,   1588, ,, 1558.

  ,, 46,   ,,   1533, ,, 1534.

CONTENTS

LECTURE I.

THE REFORMATION: ITS NECESSITY.

"Ask for the old paths."—Lev. vi. 16.

I HAVE been led to deliver these lectures because of the aggressive attitude recently taken by the Pope and the Roman Catholic Church in England, combined with the Romeward movement in the Church of England itself. In the recent Church Congress, some of the Bishops said that there was no reason to suppose that the Church of Rome was making very great progress in England. This may be, but it is very doubtful; and even if it be so, there is something far more serious than any outward aggression on the part of the Church of Rome, and that is the Romeward movement in the Church itself, which has now reached gigantic proportions. Dean Farrar has publicly stated that 7,000 of the clergy are avowed supporters of the Romeward movement. My own deliberate belief is, that he has not over-stated the number. Yet of this fact no notice, or very little, is taken by the speakers, who minimise the progress of Rome in England. One authority, indeed, did refer to some of the doctrines taught by the Romanising section in the Church with pain and censure, but it was accom-

A

panied with other observations which would go far
to deprive them of much value. It appears that
practically it is agreed on the part of many in high
places to ignore this Romeward movement, and
that the clergy are to be allowed to teach as much
of Roman doctrine and observances as they please,
and as the people will tolerate, provided always
that they are not called "Roman." Let them be
called Anglican or Catholic, primitive, or reverent,
and it is supposed that the ordinary Englishman
will not be alarmed. I am sorry to say there is too
much truth in this. I repeat, the real danger is not
Rome, but the Romeward movement from within.
Seven thousand clergy in our national pulpit,
teaching openly and constantly nearly all Roman
doctrines, and practising Roman ceremonial in our
Churches, while protesting against what they call
the "Italian Mission," and yet not exciting alarm
because the word Roman is disingenuously avoided   .
and the term Catholic used instead—this is the
alarming feature of the situation. And yet these
clergy are preparing thousands of the children of
the Church for Confirmation, when they are carefully indoctrinated in that which is substantial
Romanism, viz., the Seven Sacraments, Auricular
Confession, and the "Real Presence." It seems
almost impossible to awaken the ordinary Church-
man to any sense of the danger. Their indifference
or credulity is simply amazing and almost incredi-
ble; meanwhile our rulers in Church and State cry
"Peace and progress," and quietly discuss questions of reform, whilst the great principles of the

Reformation are rapidly being expelled from the National Church.

In the ensuing lectures, be it remembered, I am dealing mainly "with the Church of England," for it was the Church of England before the Reformation as well as since. I do not believe in the creation of a new Church at the Reformation. There has been but one Church in these lands from the beginning, even long before the sixth century. This Church has passed through various vicissitudes. First, free and independent, it was gradually, as other Churches, brought under the dominion of the Papacy, but at the Reformation the yoke of bondage was removed through God's mercy, and it regained its freedom, and what was better, the pure doctrine of the Gospel. For centuries before the Reformation it was essentially one with the Church of Rome because of the Papal Supremacy, and though the nation often fretted against the yoke and tried to cast it off by statutory enactments, *e. g.,* the Constitutions of Clarendon and the Statute of Provisors, etc., all efforts were in vain until the time of the Reformation. Alas! many seem to be going back to the house of bondage again. The Reformation was merely a crisis to which things had been tending for at least two hundred years previously. Had Luther or Henry VIII. never lived, the Reformation would have taken place under other instruments, and been brought about by other occasions. But it was a necessity. The inexorable laws which govern the course of human history must be fulfilled.

I desire now to point out briefly the need that existed, the urgent necessity which demanded such a movement as the Reformation.

I quote the following from Rev. J. Waterworth's "History of the Council of Trent: its Canons and Decrees." This is a work of acknowledged authority. Its author is a member of the order of Jesus, *i.e.*, a Jesuit, and the volume is a standard work in this Roman Catholic diocese. Waterworth admits that "the evils complained of must be encountered, and a searching remedy applied to the abuses that had crept into ecclesiastical government, to *the rank vices* that had been engendered by ages of civil wars, and to that licence and confusion which a convulsed state of society created in the discipline of the outward character of the Church." He admitted the evil of the sale of indulgences by the Popes Julius and Leo X., the cupidity and mismanagement of the agents employed, and he tells us that Adrian VI. said that his first endeavour should be to bring about "a Reformation in the court and tribunals of Rome, and that the present troubles are a just punishment from God upon the *sins of the clergy and the people*, that it was no wonder the evil had spread from the head to the members; but that he would do his best to apply remedies suitable to the occasion." (Chap. i. viii.)

But the evils were of no recent growth. Dr. Milner, a Roman Catholic dignitary (1818), not only admits the several vacancies and interregnums in the Papacy, but the unhappy schisms and rival Popes; one great one at the end of the 14th and

beginning of the 15th century, and he also admits
that "a few of the Popes, say a tenth of the number"
(about thirty), " have by their personal vices, dis-
graced their holy station." (p. 307.)
　　The evils were mainly two. 1. The Papal claims,
encroachments and usurpations on national rights.
In Henry III.'s time, the Pope claimed the revenues
of all vacant benefices, the twentieth of all Ecclesiastical revenues, a third of all above 100 marks—and a
half from all non-residents and the right to appoint
to all Bishoprics and Abbeys and large benefices.
　　The Italian clergy in England had 60,000 marks
a year—more than the entire revenues of the Crown.
Mansel, the King's chaplain, held 700 livings. The
Pope, Alexander III., annulled the Constitutions
of Clarendon in 1164, and Innocent III. annulled
Magna Charta in 1215. The former were intended
to restrain the immunities of the clergy, who refused
to be tried before the Civil Courts—the latter,
"Magna Charta," secured great liberties and advan-
tages to the Church of England, the Barons, and
the people. Pope Innocent III., from the plenitude
of his apostolic power, annulled and abrogated
the whole Charter, prohibited the Barons from
enacting it, and the King from observing it, and
absolved him and his subjects from any oaths they
had taken in reference to it, and cited the Primate
Langhton, to Rome to give an account of himself
for having anything to do with it. So we are not
indebted to the Pope for Magna Charta. 2. The
parochial clergy seem to a large extent, to have
been indolent, ignorant, and immoral. In Henry

II.'s reign, Hume says that 100 murders were committed by Ecclesiastics in a few years, and none of
them brought to justice, as they refused to be tried
in the Civil courts, and were protected in their
refusal by Thomas à Beckett and the Pope.

Let us glance at the state of things in the 15th
century, that which immediately preceded the
Reformation.   In 1509-14, there were three Popes,
Gregory XII., Benedict XIII., and John XXIII.,
each excommunicating the other.   John was com-
pelled by the Emperor Sigismund to summon a
grand General Council at Constance in 1414.   The
object was threefold : 1, to heal the schism, and
compel all to submit to one Head ; 2, to effect a
reformation both in the Head and members ; and
3, to suppress heresy.

The Council at once declared itself above Popes,
and deposed all three.   John was an awfully bad
character, guilty of every conceivable enormity and
crime.   This was acknowledged by all historians.
Martin V. was elected by the Council, and so the
schism was healed for a short time.   The Council,
however, did not forget that it was called together
to supress heresy, and accordingly severe persecution of so-called heretics followed.   John Huss
and Jerome of Prague were the first victims.   The
former was a very distinguished scholar, Rector of
the University of Prague.   He and Jerome were
disciples of John Wickliffe, or at least in part
followers of his views as a Reformer.   In doctrine
they had not gone so far, but they were strong
opponents of ecclesiastical domination, and de-

nounced the covetousness and licentiousness of the clergy. Both were condemned to be burnt, the former notwithstanding he had a safe conduct from the Emperor Sigismund. He met his death with great intrepidity. A poor woman, in her pious but mistaken zeal, showed great activity in bringing faggots to the stake ; observing which, Huss only said, " *O sancta simplicitas.*" He recognised that she thought she was doing God service. " Lord Jesus, receive my spirit," were his last words. When Jerome was fastened to the stake, the executioner offered to light the fire behind his back. "Light it before my face," was the reply, "if I had feared death I should not be here now." Both were burned at Constance in 1416.

But persecution was not confined to Bohemia. In England, in the year 1400, the Act " *De heretico comburendo*" was passed in the reign of Henry IV. In the same year, William Sawtree, priest of St. Oswith's, was burned in London for heresy. He was the first martyr that was burnt in England. A poor tailor, named Badby, was the next, at Smithfield, in 1409, and Lord Cobham, a gallant old English Knight, was hung in chains and burned over a slow fire in 1417.

The century closed with the burning of Savonarola in Florence, in 1498. He was rather a social and moral than a doctrinal Reformer. But it was quite sufficient to denounce the sins of the clergy to excite the anger of the hierarchy. He died a martyr to liberty. Alexander VI. was then on the papal throne, a monster of iniquity. He died in 1503 by poison, which he and his son, Cæsar Borgia, had prepared for another.

The sale of Indulgences.—The sale of indulgences, both before and after this period, had also a great hand in bringing on the Reformation. An indulgence purports to be a remission of a certain portion of the temporal punishment due to sin, after the guilt or eternal punishment has been remitted by the sacrament of penance, *i.e.*, confession and absolution. John XXIII. had raised money to carry on his war with the King of Naples in this way, so did Leo X. to complete the building of St. Peter's. The agents sold these indulgences in a shameless manner, offering them at various prices, and promising the purchasers, on the authority of the Pope, the remission of so many days or years from Purgatorial torment—in some cases a plenary remission was promised, which could be applied to the soul of another, if not required by the buyer. This disgraceful traffic awakened the righteous indignation of all respectable and intelligent people, and no enlightened Roman Catholic will do otherwise than condemn the abuses and scandals which thus were perpetrated in the name of religion — the demand for a Reformation therefore became more urgent.

Other causes conspired to bring about the crisis. The revival of learning by the dispersion of the Greek *littérati*, consequent on the fall of Constantinople in 1452, and the invention of printing enlightened and awakened the public conscience. Scholars began to study the Greek Testament, and

the common people the English and German trans-
lations, and thus it was discovered that the abuses
complained of—papal and clerical—as well as the
low moral tone of the people generally, arose from
"doctrinal" corruption. This was the reason why
former efforts at reformation had failed. The real
source of them lay hid, but when the intelligence
of the people was enlightened by the perusal of the
New Testament, the need of a thorough *doctrinal*
reform could alone meet the case. As long as the
Papal claims and sacerdotal pretensions were
admitted, ecclesiastical tyranny and spiritual bondage were the necessary consequences. A large part
of Christendom was now ready for the explosion—
or needed but a match to ignite the train. In the
next lecture, we shall see the commencement of the
Reformation in the Church of England under
Henry VIII.

Lecture II.

THE REFORMATION : HENRY VIII.

"N iw will I break his yoke from off thee, and will burst
thy bonds in sunder."—Nahum i. 13.

It has been said, and truly so, that the Reforam-
tion was the greatest event in history since the
establishment of Christianity. It was not an event
which took the world by surprise. Events had
been long preparing for it, and it broke out simul-
taneously, or nearly so, in all the countries of
Europe. It did not always advance gradually and
steadily, but rather wave-like, now onward, now
receding ; but, on the whole, it made progress, and
at last became an established fact. In the previous
lecture, I mentioned some of the causes which led
to it, and which finally brought it about. The need
of a reformation in morals and discipline had been
long felt, and several ineffectual efforts had been
made in that direction, but it was not until it was
realised that doctrinal corruption was at the root
of the evil, that the desired reformation was possible.
Even then, such a conviction was realised but
by few, and had to encounter enormous difficulties.
The Papacy was the buttress of the whole system ;
and it had slowly grown up and gathered strength
as the centuries rolled by. But the time had come ;

the social and moral evils had become intolerable.
The exactions of the Papacy and the clergy had
pressed heavily on the people and the nations. The
scandals of the Popes, their exorbitant claims,
their lives, together with the revival of learning
and the invention of printing, which multiplied
books, had kindled a thirst for knowledge, and
thrown light on the problem which had to be dealt
with, and also increased the demand for it.

As far as England was concerned, the first step
was to be taken by Henry VIII. He was no
Reformer; on the contrary, he was a devoted
Romanist, and for many years a steadfast adherent
of the Papacy. He was born in 1491, and was
getting on to thirty years of age when he entered
the lists against Martin Luther—writing a treatise
on the seven sacraments, in which he displayed a
very fair amount of theological knowledge and
dialectical skill. The Pope, Leo X. was delighted
with the Royal performance, and is said to have
attributed it to the special help of the Holy Ghost,
and he conferred upon Henry the title of Defender
of the Faith (*F.D.*), a title still borne by our
Sovereigns. I may mention here that the Reformation in Germany had begun a few years before this,
when Martin Luther, an Augustinian Monk, scanda-
lised by the infamous traffic of Tetzel acting for
the Pope in the sale of Indulgences, and promising
spiritual blessings for monetary payment; in 1517
affixed to the church of Wittemberg, 95 theses or
propositions against the whole theory of Indulgences. This brought down the anger of the Pope.

Luther was summoned to Rome, and, as he did
not obey the summons to appear before and submit
himself to the Pope, a Papal Bull was launched
against him, known as the Bull "*Exurge Domine.*"

Luther took the Bull by the horns, assembled his
friends, kindled a fire, and threw the Bull and the
Papal decretals into it. It is among the happiest
of my reminiscences that I have stood on the spot
where this was done. A tablet, still publicly displayed, bears the inscription—"Here Dr. Martin
Luther burnt the Pope's Bull."

But in 1526 or so, Henry begun to entertain doubts
of the validity of his marriage with Catherine. She
was the widow of his brother Arthur. They had
been married as an affair of state, to cement the
crowns of England and Spain, in 1501, when
Arthur was only 16. But he died shortly after the
marriage.

A dispensation was now sought from the Pope
by Henry VII. to enable his son to marry his
brother's wife. The Pope was not unwilling, and
the contract of marriage was entered into. But in
1505, Henry protested against the marriage, and
said he could not consent to its fulfilment. On his
father's death, however, in 1509, arguments of state
were so pressed on him that he consented, and they
were married. Two infant sons were born, but
they died. His daughter Mary alone lived. As
years rolled on, Henry was disappointed that he had
no male issue; his old scruples revived, especially
when the legitimacy of Mary was called in question
by the French ambassador. Henry said it was the

curse of God upon the marriage that he should be childless, and he applied to the Pope for a divorce. But this put the Pope in a great difficulty, for Catherine was aunt to the Emperor Charles V.; to refuse it was to vex the powerful King of England, to grant it would vex the Emperor of Germany. What were the real motives of Henry, I know not. Whether it was conscience, or passion for another, or reasons of state, or all of them combined, others must settle. I hold no brief for Henry VIII., and do not feel called upon to justify either his conduct or his character. A policy of delay was that pursued by the Pope, I suppose in the hope that time or the chapter of accidents might bring about a solution. That he could have granted the dispensation had he thought fit, is evident; it is one of the claims of the Roman Church that they have power to dispense with some of the impediments to marriage mentioned in Leviticus xviii., and to impose others additional to those that are mentioned. The weary proceedings continued for nearly seven years. At length accident, or what men call such, brought Cranmer under the King's notice. He was staying at the house of Mr. Cressy, at Waltham Cross, where Henry stopped for the night on his progress southwards. The divorce was the subject of conversation between Bishop Gardiner and Cranmer, and the latter said the best plan would be to get the opinion of the Universities of Europe on the subject—that if they pronounced that the marriage with Arthur's widow was contrary to the Word of God, no dispensation from the Pope could make it valid, and Henry was free — if they decided that the marriage was valid, the King might rest easy in his mind. This was to subject the Pope's decision to the Word of God, and involved a principle of great importance.

The King heard this, and at once exclaimed that " he had got the sow by the right ear." He sent for Cranmer, and took the course he advised. It took some years before all the answers could be obtained, but at length not only Cambridge and Oxford, but Paris, Louvain, Padua, Bologne, Ferrara, the Sorbonne, etc., all replied by majorities, more or less, that the marriage of Henry with Catherine was not lawful according to God's law, and that no dispensation could make it so.

Henry acted on this, and a private marriage took place between him and Anne Boleyn in the end of 1533. Elizabeth was born the following year, 1534. A vacancy occurring in the See of Canterbury by the death of Warham, Henry appointed Cranmer to the Archbishopric, first having obained from the Pope the necessary Bulls. I suppose he was not aware of the private marriage. But the great event of the year was the rejection of the Papal supremacy by Act of Parliament, A.D. 1534. Thus the yoke which had for so many centuries pressed so heavily on the neck of England was broken, and the burden of papal exactions removed. This act restored the national independence to the Church, and indeed to the State as well, for no State can be free or independent when a foreign potentate has the final authority in all matters which affect the spiritual welfare of the nation. At first sight it may be thought that the two domains of the spiritual and temporal are so different that the Pope might safely rule the one without interfering with the other. But this is found to be impracticable. So far from being separated, the two domains are found to interpenetrate each other. The most ordinary action in life may be found to have its spiritual side—eating, drinking, marrying, voting, ruling, all bear on spiritual things, or are influenced by them. So it was found out in practice, and the Reformation, as far as it was possible, put the Papacy out of the domain of politics. Even as it is, the influence of the Papacy, *i.e.*, of the politico-religious system which it represents, exerts through the constituences a disturbing and injurious influence on the politics of any free country, of every country where its votaries reside.

The King was proclaimed the supreme Head of the Church of England. No doubt he intended to exercise the same personal authority as the Pope had done before, for the Tudors were a sturdy race, and could brook no opposition, but all it really meant was this, that the King was the supreme governor of all estates in his realm, whether civil or ecclesiastical. The principle was that the national church, like the army and navy, should be subject to national control, and in all cases of appeal, whether doctrinal or ecclesiastical, the final award must come from the national courts and jurisdiction. This is a principle which I think no one can reasonably object to. Those who do so should withdraw from the national church. They are, happily, not obliged to remain in it.

The Pope immediately prepared a Bull of deposition against Henry, but did not publish it till 1538. It set forth that Henry had fallen from the faith and forfeited his right to the crown; it absolved his subjects from their allegiance, and put the nation under interdict; and further, Henry was denounced as a heretic, schismatic, murderer, adulterer, and rebel, who was guilty of treason against his rightful lord the Pope. He was therefore declared to be deposed, and his crown offered to the King of France or Scotland, if they would take it. Happily the Bull had no effect—the Bull had lost its thunder and its terror, for the time at least, in England, and things went on as before. The dissolution of the abbeys and monasteries followed in 1536. A visitation was ordered by Parliament, and it was found that in many instances they were little better than houses of superstition, idleness, and in some cases worse. Indeed, several had been suppressed in 1529, by Cardinal Wolsey, acting under the authority of the Pope. But in 1536 there was a final clearance made of them; nearly four hundred "religious" houses, as they were called, were suppressed, and their revenues devoted to other purposes. I have no doubt that the charges were in many instances true. It is impossible to have houses of this sort, which are free from all public inspection, without evils arising in them. It is to be regretted that such institutions are again being rapidly extended in England, not only under

Roman, but Anglican influence. They are certain to produce the same bad fruits as before. In this year, also, the Ten Articles of religion were published. These were essentially Romish as to the Rule of faith, Baptism, Sacrament of Penance or Auricular Confession, the " Real Presence " justification by Sacraments, the use of images, prayer to saints, Roman ceremonial, such as holy water, ashes, palms, candles, holy bread, creeping to the Cross on Good Friday and kissing it ; Purgatory. In 1536, however, the King ordered the Bible to be printed, and it was publicly set up in every church in 1538, for every person to read it. The Bible was, however, chained; it was not yet quite free. All the clergy were ordered to procure a copy and peruse it.

The "Six Bloody Articles" were set out in 1539. They were reactionary and sanguinary. They are as follows:—"The Real Presence," "Communion in one kind," " Clerical Celibacy," " Vows of Chastity," " Private Masses," and " Auricular Confession." Burning was the penalty attached to a denial of the first; hanging of the other five. Severe persecutions followed, and for eight years, until Henry's death, this heavy yoke was fastened on the people of England. In 1544 the Litany was set forth in English. It was drawn up by Cranmer, partly compiled out of the meagre offices of the kind already existing, but largely composed by himself. It was substantially what we have at present, saving that it contained a clause for the invocation of saints, expunged in Edward's reign.

B

It also contained a strong deprecation against the
Pope. "From the tyranny of the Bishop of Rome,
and all his detestable enormities, Good Lord deliver
us." This was expunged in Elizabeth's reign.

But the end was now approaching. In January,
1547, the King was taken seriously ill, and Cranmer
was sent for. The King was speechless. Cranmer
asked the King to give him a sign that he died in
the faith of Christ. The King pressed his hand
and expired.

The King made a will, by which he left £600 a
year for ever for the two priests of Windsor, to say
Mass at his tomb daily, and to meet some charitable
objects which he specified. I presume he feared he
might be in Purgatory a long time, and therefore
he made provision for all the remedial influences
of which such a place admits. If he were released
sooner, the benefit of the Masses would, he supposed,
do good to some other sufferer.

We can now form an estimate of the work Henry
did in reference to the Reformation. He broke the
yoke of the spiritual oppressor from the neck of the
nation, and so made reformation possible ; he
abolished the monasteries, those great supporters
of existing abuses ; he put the open Bible in the
Church. For these three things, we owe to him,
under God, a debt of gratitude. His work was
preparatory, for the most part destructive of
obstacles ; the constructive was to come. Henry
died a firm Romanist. I am not aware that he
renounced any one of the distinctive doctrines of
Romanism, save the Papal supremacy. He would

have no Popery ; but he retained all the Romanism he ever possessed.

A few words on the persecutions of his reign. They were many—beginning with Frith, and ending with Lady Jane Askew. He spared neither Protestant nor Papist. The sincere and pious Bishop Fisher and Sir Thomas More, though sincere Roman Catholics, were beheaded because they would not admit the Royal supremacy. In 1540, six men were sent to Smithfield—three Protestants to be burnt, three Papists to be hanged. They were carried on three hurdles— one of each faith on each hurdle ! William Tyndale, the famous translator of the Greek Testament (1526), was martyred in 1536, by Henry's efforts, at Villeforde, near Brussels. His last words were : "O Lord, open the King of England's eyes !" In 1538, John Lambert, an eminent divine and Reformer, was tried by Henry in person, and as he denied the so-called " Real Presence," he was ordered to be burnt at Smithfield—the scene of so many noble testimonies to Protestant truth by brave men. His last words were : " None but Christ ! none but Christ !" He suffered severely, his poor legs being burnt to the stumps before he died, the fire being insufficient, and so his agonies were prolonged.

Such was the preparation for the Reformation. We are sometimes asked : Were was your religion before Henry VIII.? We answer : Where it is now, in the New Testament. Where were its professors before Henry? Here, and in every

Christian country—persecuted, and some of them slain—Wickliffe, Cobham, Huss, Jerome. Where was your Church of England? Here, as then— but then defiled with superstition ; now, as far as our prayer books and articles are concerned, pure and scriptural. Alas ! that so many of her sons and daughters seem ready to go back to Egypt—some have arrived there already.

Brethren, let us do our utmost, by personal fidelity to the principles and the practices of the Reformation, to resist the Romeward movement, which is now threatening the very existence of the Established Church and the cause of true religion in our country.

Lecture III.

THE REFORMATION: EDWARD VI.

" In the eighth year of his reign, while he was yet young, Josiah began
to seek after the God of David his father, and in the twelfth year
he began to purge Judah and Jerusalem from the high places and
the groves and the carved images, and the molten images ; And
they brake down the altars of Balaam in his presence, and the images
that were on high above them he cut down."—2 Chron. xxxiv. 3.

I HAVE chosen this passage of the Old Testament
history, because it presents a remarkable analogy
to the conduct of our English Josiah, Edward VI.
in carrying on the work of the Reformation.

Edward was the son of Henry VIII. by Jane
Seymour, his favourite wife. She was a warm
friend of the Reformation which was then setting in.
Edward was born in 1537. He succeeded to the
throne on the death of his father in January, 1547,
and died on the 6th July, 1553, in the seventh year
of his reign, and the seventeenth year of his age.
By his will, Henry had appointed sixteen executors,
and twelve Privy Councillors, to have the charge
of the King. The Council appointed Edward
Seymour, afterward Duke of Somerset, his maternal
uncle, to be Protector of the King's person.
Somerset was a thorough Reformer, and personally
a pious, God-fearing man.

Edward's early preceptors were well qualified for

their office. They were Sir Anthony Cook, Dr. Cox, afterwards Chancellor of Oxford, and subsequently Bishop of Ely; and Sir John Cheke, Professor of Greek in the University of Cambridge. Archbishop Cranmer was his godfather. He was thus early surrounded by good influences. He was a youth of considerable talents, and became a well-informed and accurate scholar. His knowledge of the languages, both foreign and classical, was extensive, and he took the deepest interest, from his earliest years, in the theological questions which were so hotly debated around him. He was of a truly pious and religious disposition, of an earnest, devout mind, and sincerely anxious to do that which was pleasing to God. The Bible was his constant study and delight. We may well imagine that, under such tuition and training, he was intelligently and decidedly in favour of the Reformation.

At his coronation, Cranmer delivered an address appropriate to the high office to which he had been called, setting forth the duties which devolved on him, and urging him to go forward in the reformation of the Church of England. In the procession to Westminster there were carried three swords before him, emblematic of the three kingdoms over which he was called to rule. Perceiving this, he said to those by him, "There is yet one sword wanted." On enquiry being made what it was, he replied: "The sword of the Spirit, the Word of God."

Very little was done during the first year of his reign towards the progress of the Reformation, but the events in 1547 may be briefly enumerated.

First, a set of Injunctions issued early in the year, with a view to the suppression of gross superstitions, such as the adoration or excessive veneration of images, processions, the use of candles, etc. Shortly after this, it was ordered that the Epistle and Gospel should be read in English during the Mass—for the Latin Mass was still the public service of the Church. Two lessons from the Old and New Testament were to be read in English; one in the morning and the other in the evening. The First Book of Homilies, containing twelve familiar sermons on various points, was published this year, and the clergy were ordered to read them in the churches. There was need for this, for the ordinary parish priests were no preachers, nor could they be trusted, as most of them were opposed to the Reformation. The Mass was regularly performed every Sunday several times; but no sermons, save in large cities and in the principal churches. They, therefore, were very ignorant. A preaching clergy in a free land means more or less an educated clergy. The above were the principal matters effected in the direction of actual reformation; but a more important matter still was accomplished in December, 1547, viz., the repeal of the Act of the "Six Bloody Articles." As long as this Act was law, further Reformation was impossible, for it burned those who denied the Real Presence, and it hung those who denied clerical celibacy, auricular confession, or private masses for the living and the dead. At Cranmer's instance, and by his influence, this Act was repealed; and

thus the muzzle was removed from the lips of the
Reformers, and conscience was set free to speak and
act. Still the same calm deliberation marked events
in the next year, 1548, as before. One change only
of any importance waa effected, viz., the putting
forth of the "Order of Communion." This was a
short service to be added to the Mass, consisting of
one of the two exhortations in our present Book,
the confession, the prayer of humble access, and
the communication of the cup to the laity.

The next year, 1549, was an eventful one in the
history of the Church of England. The Latin
Mass, which had been used for many centuries in
this land, was abolished, and the First Book of
Common Prayer in English was substituted for it.
It came into use on Whit-Sunday, 9th June.

This Book virtually abolished the Mass and the
doctrine of the Mass. It was drawn up chiefly
by Cranmer. In seventeen particulars it struck
out phrases and expressions which distinctly taught
or implied the sacrifice of the Mass. A form
was drawn up for morning and evening prayer,
and also forms for the other offices of the Church,
Baptism, etc., etc. But though all these were a
great departure from and improvement upon the old
forms, still the Book was but partially reformed,
and contained many things which were decidedly
objectionable.

For example it contained :—

The sign of the Cross in the Communion office.

The mixed Chalice.

The Altar, and altarwise position of the Priest.

The sacerdotal vestments.

The word Mass as an alternative name for the Communion.

Auricular Confession, though left optional.

Prayers for the dead in the Communion office, and in the office for the burial of the dead.

The invocation of the Holy Ghost on the bread and wine that they might become to us the Body and Blood of Christ.

The commemoration of the B.V.M., the Patriarchs and Prophets.

Exorcism in baptism; Trine immersion; anointing the child with oil. A form of absolution appointed for private confessions, Extreme unction, reservation of the elements, etc., etc. Such was the first Book of Common Prayer. Much Roman error had been rejected, but too much remained.

This Prayer Book was followed by a new set of Injunctions, enjoining its use and forbidding certain practices, such as *"setting any candles on the Lord's Board at any time,"* and forbidding *" any counterfeiting of the Popish Mass."* Alas! what counterfeiting of the Mass in our English Churches at the present time! But we must proceed.

The year 1550 was a momentous one, and was signalised by two important events. First, the new Ordinal containing the Forms of Ordination was drawn up by order of an Act of Parliament, in which Cranmer and Ridley had the chief hand, as they had in drawing up the Book of Common Prayer. The Ordinal was to take the place of the Forms in the "Pontifical" which had been used for three or four hundred years before. The Ordaining Formula in the " Pontifical," and by which all the early Reformers had been ordained, was as follows (in Latin) :—

" Take thou authority to offer sacrifice to God, and to celebrate Masses for the living and for the dead, in the Name, etc."

These words were accompanied by the delivery of the sacred vessels into the hands of the candidates for the priesthood, and immediately on their utterance the candidates were made priests. Up to this time, they were called " Ordinandi," *i.e.,* "about to be ordained " ; now they are described as " Ordinati," " Ordained." This ordinal came into force on the 1st May, 1550, and since that date the Church of England has had no sacrificing priests, whatever vain pretensions some clergy may put forth. The Church of Rome has her sacrificing priests, or such as she regards such; she knows also perfectly well that Anglican sacrificing priests, so called, are mere pretenders, for, on what are called " Catholic " principles, Anglican orders are invalid.

The next change followed logically and theologically from the previous one—the abolition of the altars. Sacrificing priests must have altars, but as the Church had done away with the one, she had no need of the other, and so, in November, 1550, as we learn from King Edward's Journal, "orders were sent out to all the Bishops to pluck down the altars," and to substitute for them decent communion tables made of wood. How clergymen can, in the face of these two historical facts, go about professing to be sacrificing priests, and offering up the sacrifice of Christ, is a mystery to me. Surely it must be in ignorance of the facts I have mentioned.

We now pass over 1551, and come to the year 1552.

There was a growing demand for further reformation—a revision of the Prayer Book. Gardiner, Bishop of Winchester, unintentionally hastened this forward. He was a violent opponent of the Reformation, and when he came out of the Tower, where he had been imprisoned, he at once attacked the Book of Common Prayer for having rejected the doctrine of the sacrifice of the Mass in no less than seventeen important particulars ; but he also pointed out its inconsistency, in that in some ten places it still contained statements which more or less involved the sacrificial idea. He was quite right in this, for such was the case. Cranmer at once struck that weapon out of his hand by resolving on a revision, and carried it into effect ; so that everyone of those ten survivals of sacrificial doctrine, which either contained explicitly, or were capable of a 'Catholic' interpretation, was utterly expunged. Thus in twenty-seven instances the erroneous doctrine was rejected, and not a trace of the sacrificial idea left in the book.

But not content with this, all the erroneous particulars, which I mentioned as left in the first book, were also expunged, until we find the book exactly as we have it now, only with the addition of some beautiful prayers added in 1662 at the last revision.

I refer to the prayer for "All conditions of men," the " General Thanksgiving," etc. The word "altar" was also removed from the Communion office.

But besides this expurgation, other changes were made. The table was no longer to stand altarwise, as before, and, unhappily, as it always stands even now, ever since Archbishop Laud's Ritualistic innovations, but lengthwise, as was the general custom for some sixty years after the Reformation : and the minister was ordered to stand, " not afore the midst of the altar," but at " *the north side of the table,*" so that the people might see him take the bread into his hands and break it before the people, and also take the cup in like manner.

The so-called Black Rubric was also added to the Communion office, which declares that the " Body of Christ is in heaven and not here."

The general confession and public declaration of absolution at morning and evening prayer took the place of private confession and absolution, and *the permission to use the latter was withdrawn.*

There is no sufficient proof that either the first or second Book of Common Prayer was submitted to Convocation ; in fact, it is pretty certain they were not, for the majority of the bishops were opposed to the Reformation ; and so they were enacted by Parliament without convocation, and very properly. The next year, 1533, was the last of Edward's reign, but it was an important one. King Edward's Catechism was published, and all school-masters were ordered to teach it. It was the

last work of the Reformers, and contains an
admirable body of divinity, by way of question and
answer, which would furnish our younger clergy
with clear views on all doctrinal subjects, especially
those wherein we differ from Rome. Alas! they
know nothing about it.

To this was added 42 Articles of Religion, reduced to 39 in 1562. These articles contained all
our present ones, save the 5th, 12th, 29th, and 30th.
They were published in May, 1553.

Shortly after this, the King became dangerously
ill and fell into a decline. He died on the 6th of
July, and a few hours before his death he was
overheard uttering the following prayer :—

"Lord God deliver me out of this miserable and
wretched life, and take me among Thy chosen.
However, not my will, but Thy will be done, Lord.
I commend my spirit to Thee ; O Lord, Thou
knowest how happy it would be for me to be with
Thee, yet for Thy chosen's sake send me life and
health that I may truly serve Thee. O my Lord
God, bless Thy people and save Thine inheritance.
O Lord God, save Thy chosen people of England ;
O my Lord God, defend this realm from Papistry,
and maintain Thy true religion, that I and Thy
people may praise Thy holy name for Thy Son
Jesus Christ's sake. I am faint. Lord have mercy
on me and receive my spirit."

Thus the pious youthful Sovereign passed away.

A few observations in conclusion will suffice.

1. Let us praise and give hearty thanks to

Almighty God for His goodness to this nation in giving us at such a time such a sovereign, and such wise councillors to advise and guide him in the great work of the Reformation. Other nations were not so fortunate, so blessed as we. We deserved no better than they : and yet God has dealt with us more graciously than with them. " Not unto us, O Lord, not unto us, but to Thy name be the praise." Let us remember that to whom much has been given, from them will much be required.

2. How much, under God, do we owe to the Reformation? Cranmer and Ridley, and Cox, and Coverdale ; these and others, gave us the Book of Common Prayer, the 39 Articles of Religion, the First Book of Homilies, the open Bible, in a word, purity of doctrine and purity of worship, that is, wherever their teachings and rules are adhered to. Let us never forget that the very men who, with their own hands and pen, drew up the Prayer Book and the Articles, sealed them with their blood at the martyrs' fire in Oxford a few years later. We inherit blood-bought principles ; not only salvation purchased for us by the precious blood of Christ, but the Reformation, sealed by the blood of the Reformers. Ever may we hold their memories in honour, and with thankfulness to God who raised up and gave to England such men.

3. Let us train up our children in the knowledge of the facts and doctrines of the Reformation. This is our bounden duty, and it is the only safety of the nation. Let them read Foxe's Book of Martyrs, and teach them the Articles of our Church, especially

those that bear on the prevailing errors of our days. Teach them the pure way of salvation as set forth in all its simplicity in the New Testament.

4. Resist all efforts on the part of many of our clergy and laity, aye, and our political leaders also, to relax, weaken, or undo the work of the Reformation. I have not much fear of Rome without. We need not send our children to be taught religion by them. The real danger is the Romanising clergy within the Church who have the preparation of our children for Confirmation. My dear brethren, do not send your children to any such, whatever the inconvenience may be. Do not expose their tender minds to be corrupted by false doctrines.

5. Daily pray to God to influence the minds of our political rulers in the State to appoint to the Episcopal Bench only such men as are faithful to the principles of the Reformation. No man in his senses can say that this is done now. We look in vain for the appointment of such men as Cranmer and Ridley, or Latimer and Jewel. If this is not done only one result can follow. Let us, however, do all that in us lies to hand down to our children, and those that come after them, pure and scriptural Christianity, restored to us in the reign of Edward VI., that the light of the glorious Gospel of Christ may continue to shine on our highly favoured country, and by it, be diffused to the ends of the earth.

Lecture IV.

THE REFORMATION : MARY.

"The time will come when he that killeth you will think that he doeth God service."—John xvi. 2.

Mary, daughter of Henry VIII. and Catherine of Arragon, was born in the year 1516, succeeded to the throne on the 6th July, 1553, on the death of Edward VI., and died on the 17th of November, 1588, aged 43.

On the death of Edward, an abortive attempt was made by the Duke of Northumberland and the Duke of Suffolk to place Lady Jane Grey on the throne. She was the daughter of the latter, and the daughter-in-law of the former. Both were ambitious men, and as Lady Jane was of Royal blood through her mother, Frances Brandon, who was the eldest daughter of Mary, sister of Henry VIII., they persuaded Edward to appoint her as his successor ; his sisters Mary and Elizabeth having been declared illegitimate by the servile parliaments of Henry.

Edward was in declining health ; weakened in body and mind ; Jane was known to be deeply attached to the principles of the Reformation ; hence he was easily persuaded to comply with the wishes of these unscrupulous men. Their triumph, however, was but of short duration. A few days sufficed to indicate the national feeling that Mary had the best right to the throne, as the eldest daughter of Henry. The Lady Jane gladly laid down a crown which, with difficulty, she had been persuaded to assume. Mary took her place, and Jane, with her husband, was committed to the Tower. The Duke of Northumberland was executed, as was the Duke of Suffolk some time after.

Mary at once showed her opposition to the Reformation by suppressing all preaching. This has ever been the characteristic of the Church of Rome—to suppress all public discussion. In previous centuries there had been the preaching Friars, but their preaching was in accordance with the prevailing teaching of the times, and therefore there was no objection to it; but it was far otherwise with Wickliffe and his "poor priests." They met with every opposition and persecution. The Reformation was won largely by the pulpit, and it can only be effectually maintained in the same way. If the pulpit is silenced, or if the faithful ministers of Christ do not teach and expound the pure word of God, with an appeal to it only as the infallible rule of faith, and the free and enlightened use of reason as the judge of its meaning, the light of the Reformation will be quenched in darkness as before. The noble leaders of the Reformation— Cranmer, Ridley, Latimer, and others were now sent to the Tower. Towards the end of the year, viz., October, 1553, an Act of Parliament was passed repealing all the laws of Edward about religion, thus restoring the Mass, abolishing the

c

Book of Common Prayer, and bringing England back to the condition in which it was left at the death of Henry; in a word—Romanism without the Pope.

In the following year, 1554, on the 12th February, poor Lady Jane was executed. She saw the headless body of her unfortunate husband, Lord Dudley, carried across the Tower square from the block. She sent her Greek Testament to her sister, declared that she died a true Christian, hoped to be saved only by the blood of Christ, kneeled down and repeated the fifty-first Psalm; undressed, and laid her young head on the same block. Her last words were, "Lord, into thy hands I commend my spirit."

The retrograde movement was now in full operation. The Queen had sent out injunctions for the restoration of the Mass in all the Churches; and the Reforming prelates were everywhere deposed—one Archbishop and twelve Bishops. Hundreds now fled the kingdom. Arrangements were made for a disputation at Oxford between the Romanist divines and the Reformers. This took place in the month of April. Cranmer and Ridley, who were considered the most learned, were released from the Tower in order to go and dispute. The disputation lasted several days, and was conducted before Weston, Prolocutor of the Convocation. The three principal questions disputed were on the Eucharist.

1st. Whether the natural body of Christ was really in the Sacrament?

This was the doctrine of The Real Presence.

2nd. Whether any other substance did remain but the body and blood of Christ?

This was the doctrine of Transubstantiation.

3rd. Whether in the Mass there was a propitiatory sacrifice for the sins of the dead and the living?

This was the Sacrifice of the Mass.

To all these the Reformers answered in the negative, and argued accordingly. The discussion was at times very disorderly, and characterised by rude interruptions on the part of the Romish disputants, and unseemly attempts to brow-beat and jeer at the baited Reformers. At the close of the disputation, Cranmer "appealed to the judgment of God, trusting to be with Him in heaven, for whose so-called presence on the altar he was condemned."

Ridley said : "Although I be not of your company, yet I doubt not my name is written in another place, whither your sentence will send me sooner than I shall by the course of nature come."

Whilst noble old Latimer said : "I thank God most heartily that he hath prolonged my life to this end, that I may glorify God with this kind of death."

They were then judged obstinate heretics, and declared to be no more members of the Church. They were at once sent back to the Tower. In November this year, Cardinal Pole, acting as legate from the Apostolic See, invited the Parliament, in a long speech, to seek a reconciliation with the Pope. This they agreed to do, and having drawn up a supplication to that effect, they presented it on their knees to the King (Philip) and Queen, who made their intercession with the Cardinal, and on the 30th November their petition was granted. He enjoined them for penance to repeal the laws they had made against the Pope, and in the Pope's name he granted them a full absolution, which they received on their knees, and he also absolved the whole realm from all censures.

Thus England, as represented by its Parliament, was reconciled to the Pope. The Reformation was abandoned, and, to all appearance, hopelessly lost, the struggles of years frustrated, and the degradation of the nation was complete.

The Act for burning Heretics was now revived and re-enacted on the 10th December, and the fierce and terrible reign of fire and fagot, persecution, and death commenced. 1555 dawned heavily for the Reformers. I shall mention only a few of the Marian Martyrs.

On 4th February, 1555, John Rogers (Camb.) prelate of St. Paul's, who had a wife and ten children, was sentenced to be burnt at Smithfield for denying the Real Presence of the natural body and blood of Christ in the Sacrament of the Altar. The night before he suffered he drank to Hooper, who was in the same prison, and with whom he expected to be burnt. At the place of execution, the Sheriff, Woodroof, asked him if he would revoke his abominable doctrine and his evil opinion of the Sacrament of the Altar, to which he answered : " That which I have preached, I will seal with my blood.' " Thou art a heretic." " That shall be known at

the day of Judgment." "Well, I will never pray
for thee." "But I will pray for you." Then he
repeated the fifty-first Psalm—the people rejoicing
at his constancy. He was burnt to ashes, washing
his hands in the flames.

Dr. Rowland Taylor, Vicar of Hadley, in Suffolk,
was examined by Gardiner and others. Coming
away from them, he said: "God be praiséd, good
people; I am come away from them undefiled, and
will confirm the truth with my blood." He was
sent to Hadley to be burnt. His wife and family
were watching for him. An orphan girl, whom he
had brought up, said, "Mother, mother, here is my
father led away." "Rowland," said his wife,'
"where art thou." "Dear wife, I am here." They
kneeled down and prayed together. The night
before he suffered, the sheriff strongly advised him
to recant, whereupon he confessed that he had been
deceived, and was likely to disappoint many at
Hadley, viz., the worms in the churchyard, as he
would be burnt and not buried. When he was
brought to the stake, he said he had taught nothing
but God's Holy Word, and was now to seal it with
his blood. He was put into a pitch barrel, which
was set on fire, and one of the people flung a fagot
at his head. "O friend," he said, "I have harm
enough, what needeth this?" He then repeated
the fifty-first Psalm in English. And then prayed,
"Merciful Father of heaven, for Christ, my Saviour's
sake, receive my soul into Thy hands." The executioner then struck him with a halberd on the head
and killed him.

Bishop Hooper was burnt on the 9th February, 1555. He had been sent to the Fleet Prison by Mary, and had been confined there 18 months. He had denied the Real Presence of the body of Christ on the altar, and said that the Mass was an idol. He was sent to Gloucester to be burnt. Sir A. Kingston urged him to recant—"that life was sweet, and death was bitter." He replied that "the life to come is more sweet, and the death to come more bitter." His pardon was placed on a box before him if he would recant. "If ye love my soul," he said, "take it away." He was then bound to the stake, and the fire kindled, but as the wood was green, he cried out, "For God's sake, good people, let me have more fire." He was burning three-quarters of an hour. One of his hands dropped off, and he continued knocking on his breast with the other, and crying, "O Jesus, Son of David, have mercy on me, and receive my spirit," and bowing forward he died.

On the 1st of May, 1558, John Bradford was burned at Smithfield. When offered the Queen's mercy, he said, "Mercy, with God's mercy, would be welcome; but otherwise it would be none." The gaoler's wife said to him, "O, Mr. Bradford, I bring you heavy news." "What is that?" he asked. "To-morrow you must be burned." He replied, "Thank God for it, I have looked for it a long time, and now it cometh, and not suddenly. The Lord make me worthy of it." When at the stake, he said, "O England, repent thee of thy sins; beware of idolatry, beware of false Anti-

christs, lest they deceive thee." To his fellow-
sufferer, John Leaf, a youth of 19, who sprinkled
his own blood on his confession, and sent it to the
Pope, he said, "Be of good cheer, for though our
breakfast be sharp, we shall have a merry supper
with the Lord this night." He then embraced the
reeds heaped around him, and said, "Strait is the
gate and narrow the way that leadeth unto life,
and few there be that find it!" Fuller says, "He
endured the flame as a fresh gale of wind on a hot
summer day."

On the 16th October, 1555, Ridley and Latimer
endured the flames of martyrdom just in front of
Baliol College, Oxford, where now the Martyrs'
Memorial stands. They embraced each other with
great affection, and Ridley said to Latimer, "Be of
good heart, brother, for God will either assuage the
fury of the flame or give us strength to abide it."
To which Latimer replied, "Be of good comfort, for
we shall this day light such a candle in England
as I trust, by God's grace, will never be put out."
Latimer soon died, but Ridley's sufferings were
severe. He had a lingering death. There was too
much wood, and his poor legs were consumed before
the flame could break through. At length, one
opened a passage to the flames, and it put an end to
his sufferings. His last prayer was : "O, heavenly
Father, I give Thee most hearty thanks that Thou
hast called me to be a professor of Thee even unto
death. I beseech Thee, Lord, have mercy on this
realm of England, and deliver her from all her
enemies. Into Thy hands, O Lord, I commend my

spirit; Lord, receive my spirit; Lord, have mercy upon me.".

On the 21st March, 1556, the good Archbishop Cranmer suffered at Oxford. And now in St. Mary's Church he is standing, whilst Cole, Provost of Eton, preached before he was burnt. Cole urged him to confess and recant. And he began—"And now I come to the great thing that troubleth my conscience more than anything I ever did or said in my life—the setting abroad or writing contrary to the truth. And forasmuch as my hand offended, writing contrary to my heart, my hand shall first be punished; for when I come to the stake it shall be first burnt. As for the Pope, I refuse him as Christ's enemy and Antichrist, with all his false doctrines. And as for the Sacrament, I believe as I taught in my book against the Bishop of Winchester, which teaches so true a doctrine of the Sacrament, that it shall stand at the last day before the Judgment seat of God, when the papistical doctrine contrary thereto shall be ashamed to show its face."

"Stop the heretic's mouth, and take him down," cried Cole. He was pulled down and dragged out to the stake, chained thereto, and the fire kindled. He thrust his right hand into the flames and there kept it, except when wiping his face with it, that all might see it consumed before his body. At length the fire surrounded him, but he continued unmoved as the stake to which he was bound, directing his eye toward heaven, often exclaiming, "This unworthy right hand," and repeating the dying words of Stephen, "Lord Jesus, receive my spirit," till he expired. Thus died as noble a martyr, as gentle and yet as brave a soul, as ever lived on earth. He had his weaknesses, who has not? but they arose from the gentleness of his nature; his heart never wavered, and his memory will be cherished with those of Ridley, Latimer, Hooper and Farrar as five of the noblest Bishops that ever lived, and finally died, for Christ.

On the 27th June, 1556, Bonner, who was notorious for his cruelty, had thirteen persons—eleven men and two women—burnt in one fire, at Stratford-le-Bow. On the 16th of the preceding month (May) three women were burnt at once in Smithfield. In 1557, the bodies of Bucer and Fagius, two well known foreign Reformers, were dug up and burned at Cambridge—poor spite! In June, six men and four women were burnt at Lewes, in Sussex; and in September seventeen were burned in the diocese of Chichester. But I may not dwell further on these horrible cruelties. Suffice it to say that, in the four years—1555-1558—there were burnt no less than 284 persons, of whom four were Bishops, one Archbishop, twenty-one clergymen, and the rest were of all ranks, ages, sexes, and conditions.

> A noble army, men and boys,
>   The matron and the maid,
> Around the Saviour's throne rejoice,
>   In robes of light arrayed;
> They climbed the steep ascent to heaven
>   Through peril, toil and pain,
> O God, to us may strength be given
>   To follow in their train.

But the end was nigh at hand. For three years the horrible darkness of superstition and persecution overshadowed the land, save when lighted with the lurid fires of martyrdom, at Smithfield, Oxford, Gloucester, St. David's, Hadley, and Stratford-le-Bow ; but the day of deliverance was at hand by the removal of the unfortunate Queen. Her health began to fail. She was disappointed in her hopes of a family, or a successor. Her husband's neglect, and the loss of Calais, preyed on her mind ; she had no comfort in her religion, dropsy set in, and she died on the 17th November, 1558, aged only 43, a poor and heartbroken woman.

Let us take an estimate of her character. Do not suppose she was only and naturally cruel. No. She was a sincere and devout Roman Catholic, strict and moral in her life and conduct, most conscientious; hence her unrelenting persecution! She did so because she believed it was her duty. This did not make it right—far from it. She was narrow minded and bigoted, and she acted according to the light that she had. I do not say what she might have had, had she sought it aright, by prayer to God for the teaching of His Holy Spirit, and by the diligent study of the Word of God. She was full of zeal, but not according to knowledge, and the principles in which she had been brought up led her to act as she did. She acted conscientiously as did Paul when, before his conversion to Christ, he thought within himself that he ought to do many things contrary to the name of Jesus of Nazareth. Ignorance may extenuate, it can never justify, wrong doing. I have often told you that conscience in itself is not a sufficient guide. It is infallible in judging according to the rule which it recognises, but, if the rule be wrong, its decisions are wrong also. We ordinarily regulate our time by our clocks and watches, but these sometimes go grievously astray, and they require to be regulated by a chronometer that never fails, the sun. So conscience, if not regulated by reason, and, when that is not sufficient, by revelation, by the Word and Spirit of God, is bound to err. As our text says : "The time will come when they who kill you will think that they do God service." Mary was an instance of this, an instance of the awful consequences of acting according to the dictates of an ignorant, unenlightened, and misdirected conscience. Her conduct was the legitimate outcome of the principles of intolerance, in which she had been brought up. The Church of Rome holds and teaches these principles still. This, if necessary, I could easily prove by quoting from the Decrees of the Council of Trent, the Bulls of Popes, the Oath taken by the Roman Bishops, and by the syllabus published by Pope Pius IX., so recently as 1864, which teaches intolerance, denies the liberty of conscience, the free dissemination and perusal of the Bible, and asserts that the Church of Rome alone should be tolerated in Catholic countries, and maintains the right of the Church to employ force.

Other Churches have persecuted and employed severities towards those who would not obey, the Church of England, alas! not the least, in the cruel persecutions of the Covenanters of Scotland and the Puritans of England. But who justifies such actions now? We deplore them and condemn them, and are ashamed of them, and nowhere does the Church of England set forth their lawfulness. Not so the Church of Rome. She alone of all Christian communities, as far as I know, maintains the principles of intolerance. Nowhere does she go in for universal liberty of conscience, as we do, nowhere does she permit it where she can prevent it. I deeply regret this. Would that it were otherwise; but she is bound by her claims and the doctrine of Infallibility.

But I must conclude. What effect had the reign of Mary on the Reformation? In one point of view, it put it back, suppressed it, undid it. In another, it set it forward.

The Reformation was burnt into the convictions of the nation, but it was not extinguished. It was driven in, not driven out. The holy flame of truth was not quenched by the fires of martyrdom, it was simply made to burn more intensely than ever, and when the hand of the oppressor was removed it shone forth with increased brightness. The nation had learned the lesson it could not have learned in any other way—the essential intolerance of that sacerdotal system against which it was struggling to be free; and the martyrs' sufferings and the burning stake did more than a thousand sermons to make this nation a Protestant kingdom.

My brethren, teach your children the History of the Reformation, the sufferings of the Reformers, the price they paid for our privileges, and bring them up in an intelligent acquaintance with its distinctive principles, and, above all, the right, duty and responsibility of every one, our young men and maidens, boys and girls, to read, learn, live and be guided by the Word of God. And see that, under no pretence whatever, should any man or body of men come between you and its open page. The liberty we demand for ourselves we freely grant to others; equal liberty for all to serve God as his conscience directs, but without molesting or interfering with the equal rights of others.

Learn once for all the awful results which follow from the operations of an ignorant, unenlightened conscience, and that the only infallible guide of conscience is, not the Church, nor the Clergy, nor poor erring human reason alone; but the pure and uncorrupted Word of God speaking for itself. Keep it as the Lamp to your feet and the light to your path, the one Divine Rule of Faith and practice, able to make wise unto Salvation through faith which is in Christ Jesus. Conscience must be free, and no weapons be permitted but those of reason and persuasion. And ever let us cherish in deepest gratitude the noble memories of the illustrious martyrs of the Reformation who faced the fagot and the flame that we might be free; whilst for those who persecute in the name of religion let our prayer ever be—"Father, forgive them, for they know not what they do."

‸

Lecture V.

THE

REFORMATION: QUEEN ELIZABETH.

"Kings shall be thy nursing fathers, and Queens thy nursing
mothers."—Isaiah xlix. 23.

THE dark clouds which had hung over England
during the five years of Mary's reign, began to lift
on the accession of her sister Elizabeth. The fierce
fires of Smithfield and elsewhere, from which many
a noble spirit ascended in his fiery chariot, like
Elijah of old, to join the "noble army of martyrs,"
were at length extinguished, but not until they had
taught England, by an object lesson, the essentially
persecuting spirit which necessarily animates the
Papal system. I say necessarily, because the
logical result of the principles which it holds. The
nation was wearied and sickened with the awful
severities of the Marian *régime,* and now at last
breathed freely, as soon as the unhappy woman
breathed no more.

Elizabeth was the younger daughter of Henry
VIII., by his wife Anne Boleyn. She was born in
1533, and had been brought up in the principles of
the Reformation. On her accession, on the 17th of
November, 1558, the air was rent with acclamations:

"God save Queen Elizabeth; long and happily may she reign."

She was at Hatfield when her sister died, and at once set out for London. Coming to the Tower, where once she had been a prisoner by Mary's order, she fell down on her knees, and thanked God who had so graciously preserved her in her time of trouble, and, in His merciful and bountiful Providence, placed her on the throne of her ancestors.

She sent a notification, through her minister at Rome, to the Pope, informing him of her accession; but Paul IV. sent back a haughty message, that he wondered at her audacity in presuming to ascend the throne without his permission; that she was illegitimate; that England was a fief of the Holy See, etc., but that still, notwithstanding her conduct, such was the benevolent spirit of the Holy Father, that, if she humbled herself, and submitted to the judgment and will of the Pope, he would see what he could do for her. Elizabeth at once withdrew her ambassador, Sir Philip Carne.

One of her first acts was to release all prisoners for religion. A person named Rainford humbly presented a petition for the release of four prisoners who had long lain bound, whose names were Matthew, Mark, Luke and John. The Queen replied that she would first enquire from the prisoners themselves whether they desired their freedom. It is needless to ask what their reply was. The gospels were set free.

In her procession through the city, a boy representing Truth was let down from one of the triumphal arches, with a beautifully bound Bible in his hands, which he presented to her Majesty. The Queen took it with much pleasure; clasped it to her breast, and said she prized it above all other treasures.

On the 15th of January, 1559 (new style), Elizabeth was crowned at Westminster by Oglethorpe, Bishop of Carlisle, according to the form in the Roman Pontificial. None of the other Bishops would take part in the ceremony. She had already given some intimations of her intention to restore the Reformation, although she wisely refrained from anything very pronounced until the Parliament met. But she had ordered, by proclamation, that the Litany, the Epistles and Gospels of the day, and the Ten commandments should be read in English, but that no changes of ceremony were permitted until Parliament had been consulted.

The earliest Act in the New Parliament was for the restoration of the tenths and first fruits of all Benefices to the Crown, thus taking them from the Pope, to whom Mary had given them on her accession.

This Act was opposed by all the Bishops, but it passed notwithstanding. A few words here on the condition of the Episcopal Bench at this time. It was much reduced in numbers, not only by death from natural causes, but by the martyrdom of five others; and from various causes, partly her illness and troubles, Mary had not filled up their places. There were thus only sixteen Prelates, including the one Archbishop, Heath of York. Pole's death, about the same time as Mary's, left Canterbury vacant.

ALL THESE BISHOPS, WITHOUT EXCEPTION, WERE
OPPOSED TO THE REFORMATION, and not only resolved, but did their very best to prevent it ; they
stood shoulder to shoulder on their resolve ; they
spoke bravely against it in the House of Lords;
they voted against it to a man; and every act in
its favour was carried in the teeth of their open
opposition. There was only one trimmer among
them, Kitchen, Bishop of Llandaff, and he kept
out of the way. Ten Bishops out of the sixteen
were generally present at all debates, and opposed.
The remainder were either unable from illness or
distance to attend; or, perhaps, in one or two cases
thought it better not. But they were all of one
mind in opposition. They thought, if they kept
together, they would defeat the designs of Elizabeth.
Happily, they were unsuccessful, though they gave
trouble. The first opposition was, as we have seen,
in resisting the restoration of the tenths and first
fruits to the Crown.

The year 1559 was an eventful year for the
Reformation in this country, and it is well to note
carefully the successive steps as they occurred. We
have seen the first.

The Act for restoring the Royal supremacy to the
Crown, and abrogating that of the Pope, was next
under discussion. It was introduced into the
House of Lords, and vehemently opposed by all
the Bishops present, the majority of those on the
Bench. There were two or three divisions in consequence of amendments by the Commons, and on
every division they voted solid against the Royal

D

supremacy and in favour of the Pope's. The Act passed finally on the 18th March, and the Pope was ejected once more.

The Act states that it was passed by "the Queen, the Lords Temporal, and Commons in Parliament assembled," thus significantly omitting all mention of the Lords Spiritual, for it was passed, not with their concurrence, but in the teeth of their opposition. So little are we indebted to the Bishops of 1559 for the Reformation.

Shortly after this, towards the end of March, there was a public disputation held in Westminster between the Reformers and the Romanists on three points, viz., the language in which the public worship should be conducted, Latin or English; the independence of National churches, and the sacrifice of the Mass.

This was preliminary to a still further step.

The *Act of Uniformity* was now brought into Parliament and hotly discussed. It proposed to restore the second book of Edward VI., and to abolish therefore the Romish Missal. A few changes had been made in it, very few, but suggested by policy. 1. The omission from the Litany of the petition against the Pope. " From the tyranny of the Bishop of Rome and all his detestable enormities, Good Lord deliver us." This had been put in by Cranmer in Henry's time, and retained by Edward VI. But the Queen thought it calculated to give offence, and so it was struck out.

2. The declaration against the Real Presence which stands at the end of the Communion service,

commonly, but improperly called, the Black Rubric, was left out. This was done on two grounds. 1st, it was thought unnecessary, as the doctrine was virtually condemned in the 28th Article ; and 2nd, it had only been appended to Edward's Book by Order in Council, not by Act of Parliament. In this case, the Queen did not want to give offence. Her desire was to win the Romanists over to the Reformation. The motive was good, but, as usual with all weak compromises, it failed. Let me here, however, say that this so-called Black Rubric was restored by Act of Parliament in 1662, after it had been laid aside for more than one hundred years, a verbal alteration only being made, which did not alter the sense.

The third alteration was the combination into one form of the two clauses in the present formula of administration to the communicants. "The body of our Lord Jesus Christ, which was given for thee, etc." This had been in Edward's first book. "Take and eat this in remembrance, etc." This had been substituted in the second book. Elizabeth combined them both. She hoped to please both parties.

Observe, then, that with the exception of these two omissions, and this one combination or altera- tion, the book to be restored was Edward VI.'s second book pure and simple, none other, so that Elizabeth's book is Edward's book. I emphasize this, as some ignorant or designing people say that we have nothing to do with Edward's book, but Elizabeth's. The truth is, *the books are the same.*

It is the identical book we now have, with some additional prayers added in 1662.

The discussion on the restoration of Edward's book was hot and stormy. The Bishops again, true to their colours, spoke and argued bravely against it, and voted solid in opposition. But again it passed the Lords and Commons, and was enacted on the 28th April by the Queen, the Lords temporal, and Commons in Parliament assembled. The Lords Spiritual again significantly omitted, as they had neither hand nor part in its enactment. You can see this for yourselves by looking at the Act of Uniformity, which is printed in the large Prayer Book, which lies on yonder desk. There is thus the standing evidence in every Church in England that we are not indebted to the Bishops of 1559 for the English Prayer Book, and that, if they had their way, we should have the Latin Missal instead.

But some will say, they thought it was the Bishops who brought about the Reformation. There were bishops and bishops in the 16th century, as there are in the 19th. A minority of the Bishops in Edward's reign advocated the Reformation, and drew up our Prayer Book and Articles. To them we are indebted, and to Edward and his wise advisers, for the Reformation ; but not to the majority of the bishops or the clergy. The noble men who procured for us the Reformation got burned for their pains in Mary's reign, with the concurrence of the Roman prelates; and these were the men whom Elizabeth found on the bench when she came to the throne, and we have seen how they acted. Nor were the bulk of the clergy any better. The Lower House of Convocation met early in 1559, and passed five propositions in favour of the Mass, the Real Presence, Papal Supremacy, etc. Elizabeth closed the Convocation, and sent the worthy clerics about their business. The Act of Uniformity, however, passed, as I have stated, and was to come into effect on the 24th of June, 1559.

Warren's "Blackstone" says that these two Acts— the Act of Supremacy and the Act of Uniformity— are "the two links which bind Church and State together." It is a pity they are not made more of a reality than they are. They are little better, at the present moment, than a dead letter.

A set of Injunctions were now sent out by the Queen enforcing the carrying out of the Reformation through the land. The clergy were ordered to preach four times a year against the Papal Supremacy; not to extol images or relics; to preach against candles, beads, pilgrimages, and processions about the church or churchyard; to take away all shrines, candlesticks, pictures, paintings, all monuments of superstition and idolatry, so that no memory of them remain on walls, glass windows, or elsewhere. Wooden tables were to be made and set in the place where the altar stood, and so to stand, "saving when the communion is to be distributed, at which time it shall be so placed in good sort within the chancel or the church" (as ordered later by the 82nd canon) "as that the minister may be more conveniently heard; and after the communion to be put back where it stood before."

But we must pass on. As a consequence of the Act of Supremacy it was necessary that the oath of allegiance embodying that Act should be put to and taken by the Bishops individually. The Bishops resolved to refuse, and to stand together; for if they did the Queen would be obliged, they thought, to give in, as she could not carry on the episcopal succession without them. The testing process now began. The oath was offered to three or four of the Bishops. They refused—and were at once deposed. A month later it was proposed to four or five more. They also refused and were deposed. Another breathing space. It was offered to half a dozen more; they stood firm and were deposed. At last, one bishop alone remained on the bench, the well known old trimmer, a genuine Vicar of Bray, Kitchen, Bishop of Llandaff. He alone of the fifteen or sixteen prelates took the oath and retained his see. Thus Elizabeth made a clean riddance of all the recusant Bishops, and poor Kitchen sat alone. What will the Queen do now? She was not without her resources.

There were five Bishops in England who had been deposed by Mary—Barlow, Scory, Coverdale, Hodgkins, and Salisbury. Kitchen, too, was to be had, and behind all these stood the unbroken ranks of the Irish Bishops, for these worthy men, no doubt from excellent motives, had all, with only two exceptions, the Bishops of Meath and Kildare, twenty-two out of twenty-four, conformed to the

Reformation, so that Elizabeth had abundance of materials by the aid of which she could reconstitute the desolated English Episcopal Bench.

She issued a commission to the first five named, together with Kitchen, and the Bishop of Ossory (Bale), directing that they or any four of them should consecrate Dr. Matthew Parker, of Corpus Christi College, Cambridge, to the Episcopal office. This, though not without some delay, was accordingly done on the 17th December, 1559, in Lambeth Chapel, by the four Bishops, Barlow, Scory, Coverdale, and Hodgkins. Kitchen, if he did not actually refuse, managed to evade the unpleasant office.

Parker was duly consecrated according to our English form. The Roman Catholic historian, Dr. Lingard, says that two of the four, Barlow and Hodgkins, had been consecrated according to the Roman Pontifical, and the other two by the Edwardine Ordinal, and that of this consecration there can be no doubt. Some doubts have of late been thrown on Barlow's consecration. But even if so, it would not invalidate Parker's. All the four placed their hands on his head, and all repeated the words of ordination. At the same time, we must never forget that the New Testament prescribes no form of words whatever for any ordination, and only mentions, as a fact, two things— prayer and the laying on of hands, as used by the Apostles ; but what the prayers were is not recorded. Of the validity of Parker's ordination or consecration, I entertain no doubt. That it was strictly canonical, *i.e.*, according to the ancient canons, I do not maintain, for the consecrating Bishops had no sees at the time, and this was, therefore, uncanonical. But canons have only human authority, and can be abolished, altered, or dispensed with, by the same authority that enjoined them, viz., the Church or Christian society.

The work of re-construction now set in apace. The Bishops who had consecrated Parker, at least three of them, were appointed to sees. The others were filled up by sound Protestant Divines selected by the Queen, and consecrated by Parker and his assistants, and thus the old ship of the National Church was manned once more, and better manned than it had ever been before, or since.

We now pass on to 1562, about two years later than the events of 1559.

A Convocation was summoned to meet in London to deal with the Articles of the Church. The 42 which Edward had left, and which Mary rejected, were subjected to a careful review and revision. They were reduced in number to 39. Some seven were laid aside, and four new ones, viz., 5th, 12th, 29th, and 30th of our present Articles were agreed to, thus making the number which we now have. Some important additions were made to the 25th, condemnatory of the five additional sacraments of Rome, also a clause in the 28th ; teaching that the presence of Christ in the Lord's Supper is only a presence to faith, not an objective presence independent of faith.

These Articles were ratified again in 1571, and so

they have stood without one letter of alteration for the last 325 years, a splendid body of divinity, 39 pillars on which the Protestantism of the Church of England firmly rests. All we need is a living body of faithful clergy, who will take, and believe, and teach the 39 Articles in their literal and grammatical sense ; and in all the greatness and depth of their spiritual signification. The Second Book of Homilies and Jewel's Apology were approved by the same Convocation.

Please observe that these Articles were not submitted to the Convocation until the Episcopal Bench had been cleared of its Romanizing prelates, and their places supplied by sound Protestant Bishops. And this is a lesson, an object lesson of what ought to be the policy of our rulers in the state at the present day. Queen Elizabeth could act with a high hand, and she did. Queen Victoria cannot; the responsibility rests with her constitutional advisers. Let them appoint only Protestant Bishops, *i.e.*, men faithful to the principles of the Reformation.

I must now rapidly touch the principal events of Elizabeth's long and eventful reign as bearing on the Reformation.

In 1569, Pious V. issued a Bull against Elizabeth, deposing her from the throne, and exciting her subjects to rebel. It was affixed to the door of Lambeth Palace by one Felton, a Romish seminarist. He was taken in the fact, and executed for treason.

In 1572, the awful Massacre of St. Bartholomew

in Paris, when some 70,000 Protestants were murdered, among whom was Admiral Coligny the Huguenot. The Queen refused to receive the French Ambassador. Pope Gregory XIII. struck a medal commemorative of the event, and sang a *Te Deum* for joy. He also, in 1575, and 1578, issued two Bulls against Elizabeth, addressed to the Irish rebels, and stirring them up against her.

In 1588, the abortive Spanish Armada was sent against this country under the blessing of Pope Sixtus V. Happily the design was defeated by the bravery of English sailors, and the manifest interposition of Almighty God by his winds and waves.

In 1591, the famous University, of which it is the proudest honour of my life to be a graduate, Trinity College, Dublin, was founded by Elizabeth to raise up a faithful and learned ministry, and to diffuse the principles of the Reformation in Ireland. This duty it has well fulfilled, and one need only mention the names of Usher and Berkeley, Swift and Bramhall, the Magees—grandfather and grandson—McNeile, Elrington, Lee, and others, not to mention the present learned, and modest as well as learned, Provost Dr. Salmon, equally celebrated as a theologian and a mathematician. It is the one institution of which all Irishmen are proud, and had- not its influence being thwarted by well-meant, but unwise, political action on the part of our rulers, Ireland would have long since ceased to be a thorn in the side, or source of trouble to England.

In 1601, Clement VIII. issued a Bull against Elizabeth. Thus for forty years the Papal authorities never ceased to harass that great Queen, and compel her in self-defence to adopt measures of severity against the emissaries of rebellion and treason. She had been deposed, as far as Papal Bulls could do it, by four Popes, and the consequence was several attempts on her life, and her dominions offered to any potentate who could take them. Motley says, "She was no advocate for religious liberty, nor had she the faintest idea of it. It would, however, be unjust in the extreme to overlook the enormous difference in the amount of persecution exercised by the Protestant and Roman Church. It is probable that not more than 200 Catholics were executed as such in Elizabeth's reign, and this was ten score too many.

"But what was this against 800 heretics burned, hanged, and drowned in the Easter week by Alva, against the 18,200 sent to the stake and scaffold, as he boasted, during his administration, against the hundreds of thousands who perished by the edicts of Charles V. in the Netherlands, or in the single St. Bartholomew massacre in France? Moreover, it should never be forgotten that most of the Catholics who were executed in England suffered rather as conspirators than heretics. She had been denounced by the Pope as a bastard and usurper, her subjects had been released from the bonds of allegiance, and a crown of glory promised to those who should succeed in depriving her of life. Yet this was the position of Elizabeth. It was war to the knife between her and Rome, declared by Rome herself, and the seminary priests who came to

England were a perpetually organised band of conspirators and assassins." (Vol. ii., pp. 276-277.)

Elizabeth died on the 24th March, 1603, in her 70th year, having reigned 45 years. She was a great woman ; she had a masculine intellect, and a woman's vanity, without her amiability. She was a great stateswoman ; an able ruler. She could hold her own with the kneenest statesman of her age. She was great ; was she also good? I cannot tell. She was, as I have said, vain, and I do not think she had much of the softness of her sex. But she loved England, and died a virgin Queen, having defied and defeated all the efforts of Spain and the Pope ; sitting on her island rock, enshrined in the loyalty of her subjects—the Mistress of the Sea. Her reign was glorious—an outburst of national greatness which has never been surpassed. She was served by able men—admirals, generals, statesmen, and philosophers. Whatever may have been the faults of her personal character, she did a work for England which we can never sufficiently appreciate. She rescued the nation from the grasp of the Papacy, and restored and consolidated the Reformation. Her end was a sad one ; she fell into a state of melancholy, chiefly because of the execution of the Earl of Essex, to which she had consented, and to whom she was attached. She fell into a lethargic condition, and passed away in the 70th year of her age, and the 45th year of her reign. "So dark a cloud overcast the evening of that day," says Hume, "which had shone out with a mighty lustre in the eyes of all Europe."

Let us thank God for our own gracious Sovereign, Queen Victoria, who has reigned for a much longer period, and who has all the wise statesmanship and intellectual qualities of Elizabeth ; and, in addition, all a woman's heart, full of sympathy and compassion for every phase and case of sorrow and suffering. Her own heavy trials and sorrows have endeared her to all her subjects, and she truly lives enshrined in their love and esteem. She loves the Bible, and has declared that to it England owes its greatness. May she be long spared to us, and when the earthly crown is worn no more, may she inherit, through the merits of our Redeemer, the crown of glory that fadeth not away.

LECTURE VI.

WHAT WE OWE TO THE REFORMATION.

"Our soul is escaped as a bird out of the snare of the fowlers:
the snare is broken, and we are escaped."--Psalm cxxiv. 7.

WE have now completed our sketch of the English
Reformation in the 16th century from an historical
point of view, and we have seen how it was worked
out during four successive reigns, those of Henry
VIII., Edward VI., Mary, and Elizabeth. The
need of such a Reformation was dealt with in the
first lecture; the successive stages in the four which
followed. Its progress was not uniformly onward,
at least in outward manifestations.

Henry VIII. simply made a Reformation possible,
and did little more. He made it possible by the
overthrow of the Papal supremacy in this country.
As long as that was acknowledged, Reformation
was an absolute impossibility. The interests of the
Papacy and its adherents were against it. The
abuses and doctrinal errors were essential to its
existence. The translation of the Bible and its
perusal by Henry's permission helped the Reformation, and furnished men with a definite Rule of
Faith. The dissolution of the Abbeys and Monasteries still further promoted the changes that were

impending, but nothing more was done. No changes of either doctrine or worship were attempted, and the Latin Mass, Masses for the dead, auricular confession, and absolution, were in full force till Henry's death. He died as he lived, a Romanist.

The Reformation was effected in the following reign, that of Edward VI., not, indeed, all at once, but with marvellous despatch. At first, partially by the Book of Common Prayer, 1549—completely by the Second Book in 1552. The Latin Mass was abolished; the English Liturgy and the Articles of Religion were adopted.

Mary's reign was reactionary, a step backward. The Reformation was rejected; Romanism and the Papal Supremacy were restored. But, though this was done, as far as the action of the governing authorities were concerned, yet the Reformation itself, the principles of the Reformation, were burnt into the mind, heart, and conscience of the people by the fires of Smithfield and Oxford, and thus Mary's sad and cruel reign was really helpful rather than otherwise. The nation learnt more in those five years of persecution what Romanism really is than could possibly have been learned in any other way.

On Mary's death, the nation, under Elizabeth, gladly welcomed the Reformation once again. . She restored the English Liturgy and rejected the Papal supremacy in despite of the most strenuous opposition of every Bishop on the Bench, and having deposed them and filled their places with truly Protestant Bishops, the work of reconstruction and consolidation was successfully accomplished. Many people imagine that the Bishops, in 1559, approved of the restoration of the Reformation, and even helped to restore it. This is a complete mistake. The Reformation was restored in despite of all the Bishops, and the opposition of Convoca. tion.

This evening, I shall try and gather up as briefly as I can, the net results of that wondrous religious revolution, and enquire :—

What do we owe to the Reformation? What its outcome, what its blessed consequences?

First, the Open English Bible.

That is, the Bible in the vulgar tongue, with free permission to read it. Not only the permission, but the duty and responsibility of doing so ; and being guided by it in our faith and practice.

This the Church of Rome does not permit. By the fourth Rule of the Index—the standing law of that Church, the indiscriminate reading of the Bible is condemned, and no Roman Catholic is allowed to read it without a written permission from the Ecclesiastical authority. I do not say this rule is always acted on in this country; very probably it is not. For this relaxation, there are, no doubt, excellent reasons—one is the difficulty of its enforcement in a free country ; but I have nothing to do with that, I am merely stating the actual law of that Church. Besides, the Church of Rome does not hold that the Bible only is the rule of Faith;

she adds thereto, tradition, and superadds the
Church as the final and infallible interpreter of the
Bible. The Reformed Church of England, on the
other hand, declares in the Sixth Article that "Holy
Scripture containeth all things necessary to salvation ; so that whatsoever is not read therein, is
not to be required of any man that it should be
believed as an Article of the Faith, or be thought
requisite or necessary to salvation." And, in the
first Homily, the diligent reading of the Word of
God is urged on all. The Bible is the infallible
rule of Faith and practice, and the Holy Ghost is
promised to every one who asks, and He is the
Infallible Guide and teacher of the faithful, leading
them into all necessary truth—necessary to salvation.

SECOND, THE PURE GOSPEL.

The Reformation restored the Gospel in all its
purity, unmixed with superstition or human error
of any kind—God's method of salvation as stated in
His written word. First, the Divine Remedy ; the
only merit of our Lord and Saviour, Jesus Christ ;
His spotless Righteousness, His precious blood,
His finished work on the Cross. One offering, once
offered ; once for all. This is in opposition to the
Roman Mass, which maintains that the offering of
Christ is "daily renewed" by the Priest at the
altar. Secondly, the one and only means whereby
the merit of Christ is applied to our individual
souls, viz., by Faith and Faith only. This is in
plain opposition to the teaching of the Church of
Rome, which is, that Faith alone is not sufficient

E

to justify without the Sacraments ˙ and good works.

THIRD, DIRECT ACCESS TO THE THRONE OF GRACE, without the necessity of priestly intervention.

This is the privilege of every believer in Christ. " Having, therefore, brethren, boldness to enter into the Holiest by the blood of Jesus ; . . and having a High Priest over the House of God, let us draw near with true heart, in full assurance of faith." And again, "Let us draw nigh with boldness to the Throne of Grace, that we may obtain mercy and find grace to help in every time of need." The Church of Rome, on the contrary, teaches the ordinary necessity of the Sacrament of Penance, *i.e.*, auricular Confession, and sacerdotal absolution, in order to reconcile sinners to God. The Reformation proclaims the non-necessity of any confessional whatever, save that which the penitent sinner can at all times enter, by personal application to Christ, and receive at once from His own gracious lips the blessing of a frank, free, and full absolution, with grace and help to sin no more.

What a contrast is this Gospel plan of salvation to the whole system of sacramentalism which is taught alike by Romanist and Ritualist. Both alike maintain "that Christianity is a religion of sacraments—its beginning is sacramental ; its middle is sacramental ; and its end is sacramental. Every intervening step is sacramental, and not a single step can be taken in the divine life without the co-operation of sacraments." That is, without the co-operation of priests ; because there are, they say, seven sacraments, of which Order is one ; and the sacerdotal order is necessary to the validity of all the sacraments, Baptism only excepted in exceptional circumstances. This sevenfold chain of sacramental bondage is snapped asunder by the doctrine of the Reformation.

FOURTH, PARADISE INSTEAD OF PURGATORY.

This we owe to the Reformation. The Council of Trent teaches that there is a Purgatory for the expiation and purification of the souls of the faithful from those stains which have not been wholly removed on earth ; and that the souls therein detained are relieved whilst there, and their sufferings shortened by the suffrages of the faithful, and principally by the Holy Sacrifice of the Mass.

The Reformation denies, on the authority of Holy Scripture, that there is any Purgatory whatever, and declares, on the testimony of Christ, that the believing soul, on its separation from the body, immediately enters Paradise, and, on the authority of St. Paul, that "to depart is to be with Christ, which is far better." That, whilst to live is, to the believer, Christ ; to die, is not pain in Purgatory, but gain. Hence, all prayers for the dead were expunged from the Prayer Book in 1552, and instead thereof, thanksgiving and praise were inserted in 1552 and 1662. We may now say, "Blessed are the dead which die in the Lord." "O Death, where is thy sting?" "O Grave, where is thy victory?"—Thanks be to God who gives us the victory through our Lord Jesus Christ.

FIFTH, THE REAL PRESENCE OF CHRIST IN THE HEART OF THE BELIEVER AT ALL TIMES.

This, instead of the real presence of His body and blood on the altar, we owe to the Reformation.

Before that glorious emancipation, the Church of England, in common with the Church of Rome, held that the real body of Christ was objectively present on the altar, after the consecration of the wafer, independent of faith. The Reformation taught us otherwise. To it we owe the scriptural truth, that "the Body of Christ is in heaven, and not here." That the bread and wine on the Table are simply the emblems of His blessed body and blood; the pledges of His love, and a precious means of grace to "all who rightly, worthily, and with faith receive the same." We do not deny the real presence of Christ in the true and Scripture sense—that is, that Christ is really present in grace and blessing, where two or three are gathered together in His name; yea, that He is present in the hearts of His faithful people, and will never leave them nor forsake them, but will be with them to the very end of the world. But we utterly repudiate, with the Reformers, the presence of His body and blood on the Lord's table. They are at the right hand of God, and will there remain until He comes to judge the world.

SIXTH, THE CHRISTIAN MINISTRY.

To the Reformation we owe the restoration of the Christian Ministry, instead of a sacrificing priesthood. For several hundred years before the Reformation, the Church of England, under Roman influence, held that the clergy were sacrificing priests —they were ordained as such—and, in their ordination, received a commission "to offer sacrifice to God, and to celebrate Masses for the living and the dead"—in a word, to offer the sacrifice of the Mass, which the Church of Rome teaches is "truly propitiatory," and one with the sacrifice of Christ.

This doctrine was utterly repudiated by the Reformers in 1550. Every trace of a sacrificial element was carefully expunged from the Communion office, and the Ordinal, or form of ordination; and the clergy were declared to be simply "watchmen, stewards, and messengers" of the Lord. They were no longer to be sacrificing priests; but preachers and pastors, conducting the public worship of the Church; ministering the two Scriptural sacraments which had been retained out of the pre-Reformation seven; but, above all things, they were to be ambassadors for Christ, preaching the everlasting Gospel, the true key of the Kingdom of Heaven ; and, as a teaching ministry, by the exposition of the Word of God, to edify the body of Christ. ·

The word "priest" in the Prayer Book simply means, as is known to every scholar, an elder—it is the contraction of the word presbyter. The word which means a sacrificing priest, and which is applied to the Jewish priests and the Pagan priests in the New Testament, is never once applied to the Christian minister, though some ten other titles of office are given to them. The Christian ministry is no longer a celibate priesthood, but a married clergy, as were the divinely appointed priests of the Old Testament, and are thus united to their people by all the common ties of citizenship and family relationship: for, as the late Prince Consort once said, "The people felt that their newly-acquired civil and religious liberties would not be safe in the hands of any other than a married clergy, who move in and out among their people, the sharers and sympathisers of their joys and their sorrows."

SEVENTH, THE TRUE IDEA OF THE CHURCH.

This, also, we owe to the Reformation—we no longer confound the Church visible and the Church invisible as in all respects one. We distinguish between the Church mystical and the mere outward body. The former is the "blessed company of all faithful people." They constitute the mystical Body of Christ; they are united to Him the Head by the indwelling of the Holy Spirit. They are regenerated, renewed and sanctified; "they are conformed to the image of Christ; they walk religiously in good works; and, finally, by God's mercy, they attain to everlasting felicity."

We do not confound this spiritual body of Christ, consisting of all true Christians in all Christian communities, with the aggregate of visible churches, still less with any one of them. All visible churches are mixed bodies, consisting of good and bad. To the former alone belong the promises, as they alone are partakers of the Life of Christ. The Church of Rome claims to be exclusively the Church of Christ, whereas, she is only a part, and, as we believe, a very corrupt part of the visible Church. Her doctrine is that Christ's true Church is always visible as such ; united, not only by a common faith, but also under one special form of Government, and one visible head — the Pope, who is, they say, the successor of St. Peter, and the Vicar of Christ; that this Church is infallible, as is its visible head; to it, and to it alone, belong the promises; all others who profess the Christian religion are heretics or schismatics, or both ; they are, at least, non-Catholics.

The Reformation wholly rejected that view, and teaches that all who are renewed by God's spirit, who love Christ and follow the blessed steps of His most holy life, are true Christians, and alone constitute the Holy Catholic Church. This we maintain is the true scriptural idea of the Church of Christ. In the present dispensation, the true and the mere professors are mixed together in one outward body, the tares and the wheat, the wise and the foolish, the good and the wicked ; sometimes the bad and the worldly are in a majority, and therefore the whole visible Church may err, and has erred in parts, more or less, as did the seven Churches of Asia, etc. But in the darkest seasons, God has a faithful remnant, as the seven thousand in the time of Elijah. These, and these alone, are properly His

Church. At the end of the dispensation, a separation
will take place ; Christ will send forth his angels to
gather together his elect, to take out of his kingdom all that offend. Then shall the righteous be
manifested and the blessed company "shall shine
forth as the sun in the Kingdom of their Father."

EIGHTH, PURITY OF WORSHIP.

This also we owe to the Reformation. Before that
event the public worship of the Church was as is
that of the Church of Rome now. It was an
elaborate and minute ceremonial ; histrionic in its
character—*i.e.*, an appeal rather to the eye than
to the ear—a religious performance, in fact. The
sacred office of the Mass was the chief service of
.the day, consisting largely in action, bowing, genu-
flection, elevation, prostration, censing, lighted
candles, etc. The service itself purported to be a
representation of the sufferings of our Lord. The
words were uttered in Latin, most of them with
the face turned from the people, and the more
sacred and. solemn parts in a very low tone, so as
to be wholly inaudible. I am willing to believe
that they were perfectly sincere in this service, and
believed it to be what God approved of, but inten-
tions cannot alter facts, or make them to be other
than. they are. The Reformation abolished all that,
rejected the Mass and the doctrines whereon it
rested, and completely altered the character of the
public worship, substituting for it the plain scriptural, simple, and, as we believe, spiritual services,
which are prescribed by our Church, in which the

ear is appealed to, rather than the eye ; the reason and the understanding, rather than the emotion and the imagination.   The pulpit is prominent, not the altar ; the common and united worship of the people in the vulgar tongue, rather than the cele-bration of sacred rites before them by a sacerdotal order in a language not understanded of the people.

NINTH, LIBERTY, CIVIL AND RELIGIOUS.

The great result of all the foregoing, procured for us by the Reformation, was liberty—spiritual, in-tellectual and political—freedom in its widest extent; liberty, not license ;   the sacred rights of the individual conscience; the frank and full recognition of the right of every man to think for himself, and to worship God as he believed right, but without interfering with the equal rights of others.   This is not admitted by the Church of Rome.

This glorious freedom was not indeed fully rea-lised or exercised all at once.   It took well nigh a hundred years before the victory was won ; and, in fighting that battle, we must never forget what we owe to the Covenanters of Scotland, and the Puri-tans of England.   But though the struggle was long, the victory was involved in the very first principle of the Reformation—the open Bible, and the right of every man to read it for himself.

To this great principle I attribute the greatness of Great Britain, the mother of free peoples; and that principle has placed her at the very top of imperial sovereignty.   Sacerdotalism enslaves and cramps the human mind.   The open Bible and the sacred rights of conscience emancipate and ennoble it. The superstition of the middle ages dwarfed and degraded; the Reformation restored manhood to the Protestant nations of Europe.

Thus have I put before you some of the chief blessings which we owe to the Reformation :—

1. The open Bible.
2. The pure Gospel.
3. Direct access to God.
4. Paradise instead of Purgatory.
5. The real presence in the heart, not on the altar.
6. The Christian Ministry, not a sacrificing Priesthood.
7. The true idea of the Church.
8. Purity of public worship.
9. Liberty—civil and religious.

Thus was accomplished what Burnet says was the design of the Reformation—"To restore Christianity to what it was at the first, and to purify it from the errors which had sprung up in the dark ages." This it did, and more; for the Gospel has the promise of the life that now is, as well as of that which is to come. It gave national prosperity, freedom, civilisation, empire.

A few words in conclusion. It is a sad reflection that these blessings of the Reformation are now seriously jeopardised in this glorious country of ours. In thousands of our national Churches they have actually ceased to exist; and the work of the Reformation is undone. There has been an extraordinary and alarming recrudescence of Romanism in the Church of England, among her clergy and her people, during the last fifty years; and thousands of her churches have been captured for Rome, and the "counterfeit of the Mass," has been again set up, and many of our rulers in Church and State are its advocates and sympathizers. The mass of the people of England seem indifferent or aquiescent. They do not realise the danger. If anything could open their eyes to the Romeward movement within and without the Church, one would think the recently published life of Cardinal Manning, by a sincere Roman Catholic, would do so; when we find that for five years, at least, before he left the Church of England, he spoke (to quote the words of his biographer),

"WITH A DOUBLE VOICE."

In public and to his penitents, he professed his undying confidence in the Church of England; and maintained an anti-Roman attitude; and yet in his diary, and to his intimate friends, he declared that he had ceased to believe in that Church, as she had gone astray from the Catholic Church, both organically and functionally. What an awful revelation of the inconsistency of human nature; and yet he thought he was doing right all the time !

In conclusion. . What is our duty in reference to the present crisis?

1. Parents: see that your children are carefully and intelligently taught the historical facts, and the distinctive principles of the Reformation as I have endeavoured to place them before you in these lectures.

2. Do not send your children to be prepared for Confirmation by any clergyman whom you do not know to be loyal to the Reformation; lest you may find them taught in the necessity of Auricular Confession and Priestly Absolution.

3. Young men and women, make yourselves acquainted with the facts and principles I have set forth. Do not take them merely on my representation, or that of any other clergyman. Consult original authorities yourselves. Read the Articles and Homilies of the Church of England. Read the works of the British Reformers—Cranmer, Ridley, Latimer, Jewel, Edward VI., or Foxe's Book of Martyrs, published by the Religious Tract Society. You can get them for two shillings a volume. Do not grudge the time. It is well worth the trouble.

4. Do not countenance by your presence, merely because of convenience, churches where the Romeward movement is in any degree promoted; better worship God at home in your closets, though better still to get others to join with you and plead the promise of Matt. xviii. 20.

5. Help both financially and by personal effort every wise movement for the defence and diffusion of Reformation principles. Don't be ashamed to take your open stand on that side in these testing days.

6. Above all; be constant in daily prayer that God may open the eyes of the rulers and people of England before it be too late; and to overrule the designs, deliberations and decisions of mere worldly

politicians to the extension of true religion and the overthrow of ignorance and superstition.

Let our motto' be—

The Bible only.

Jesus only.

Faith only.

The Bible the only Rule of Faith; Jesus the only object of Faith, the only priest, the only offering, once offered on the Cross, finished there.

Faith the only hand that puts on Christ, the link that binds us to Him, that works by love, purifies the heart, and overcomes the world.

THE END.

BY THE SAME AUTHOR.

THE BOOK OF BERTRAM: *de Corpore et Sanguine Domini.* **1/-**

WHY SHOULD WE BELIEVE THE BIBLE? OR REASONS FOR FAITH. **1/-**

THE ROYAL SUPREMACY OVER THE CHURCH OF ENGLAND. **6d.**

ANGLICAN ORDERS. **1/-** per dozen.

IS CHRIST NOW OFFERING? A Paper. **6d.** per dozen.

MIRACLES. An Essay. **3d.**

"WHOM WE PREACH." An Ordination Sermon. **4d.**